The Open Window

poems by

Mary M. Sesso

Finishing Line Press
Georgetown, Kentucky

The Open Window

for my son, Eric

Copyright © 2018 by Mary M. Sesso
ISBN 978-1-63534-387-8 First Edition
All rights reserved under International and Pan-American Copyright Conventions.
No part of this book may be reproduced in any manner whatsoever without written permission from the publisher, except in the case of brief quotations embodied in critical articles and reviews.

ACKNOWLEDGMENTS

Acknowledgements are gratefully extended to the journals in which these poems first appeared, sometimes in variant form.

Coal Hill Review: "Garden Of Choices"
Chest: "The Heart Rate You See on the Monitor May Not Be Accurate"
Comstock Review: "Saying I'm Sorry after the Quarrel," "Hand-Speaking," "Carbon"
Helen Literary Magazine: "When the Day Lilies Open"
Homestead Review: "Mad Red Sunset," "Sailor"
GFT: "The Drums Argue," "The Large Baby Doll"
Gyroscope Review: "The Open Window," "Sometimes a Body Is Just a Body"
Medical Literary Messenger: "Broken"
Passager: "I Was Going to Write"
Ship of Fools: "Young Boys Watch Helentroy Diamond Jones"
Third Wednesday Literary Journal: "Migraine"
White Pelican Review: "Francis Goya: Don Manuel Osorio de Zuniga", "Persistence, 1956"

Publisher: Leah Maines
Editor: Christen Kincaid
Cover Art: Pixaby.com CC0 Creative Commons
Author Photo: Alexis Paza
Cover Design: Elizabeth Maines McCleavy

Printed in the USA on acid-free paper.
Order online: www.finishinglinepress.com
also available on amazon.com

Author inquiries and mail orders:
Finishing Line Press
P. O. Box 1626
Georgetown, Kentucky 40324
U. S. A.

Table of Contents

A Garden of Choices 1
Always 2
When the Day Lilies Open 3
Cancer School 4
After He Left 5
Young Boys Watch Helentroy Diamond Jones 6
Frances Goya, Don Manuel Osorio de Zuniga 7
Weather Alert 8
The Binge Drinker's Daughter 9
The Large Baby Doll 10
2 West 12
Ypsilanti State Hospital, 1951
    1. Vamping 13
    2. Hydrotherapy 14
    3. Treatment Plan 15
    4. Jesus Catches the Light in His Hand 16
The Open Window 17
Riding a Red Bicycle 18
No Exit 19
Carbon 20
Persistence, 1956 21
Broken, 1970 22
Sailor 23
Mad Red Sunset 24
The Heart Rate You See on the Monitor May Not
Be Accurate 25
In a Perfect World 26
Sometimes a Body Is Just a Body 27
The Drums Argue 28
Saying I'm Sorry after the Quarrel 29
Migraine 30
Hand-Speaking 31
I Was Going to Write 32

*The truth is not always beautiful,
nor beautiful words the truth.*

Lao Tzu

Garden of Choices

It all comes down
to my friend telling me
he's an empty basket.
Why not fill it, I ask,
with the dead of night,
the wet light of morning
or maybe a sigh?

Next, a layer of sound—
the bark of an unseen dog,
song the cricket hauls
to my porch to drown out
the tyranny of thunder,
and the murmur of wildflowers
as frost hovers.

Then you could weave
across the basket handle
the hiss of a slingshot stone
speeding past your ear,
the shiver from its closeness
and the splendor of a spark
as stone strikes stone.

Always

There is always a woman,
orchid pretty like a lady slipper,
a rare flower, tucked away
in the woods, struggling
to hang on undisturbed,
dreaming of an easier life
in a world too busy nattering
to care.

Or a woman kneeling to pick
dandelions around the grave
of her baby feels a coldness
creeping around her body,
wishes a heat could hug her
so delicious she would
dance into heaven happy.

Or a woman holding a bouquet
of wild violets, pressing
the smallest one close to her chest,
measuring between her finger
and thumb the delicate blossom
and storing the touch to take
with her if an early winter
covers the earth with snow.

When the Day Lilies Open

She awakens sleep-deprived
on the oncology ward
offended by the cloudy light
that's opening the day lilies
in her back yard.

Cancer has again pruned away
dreams not about itself—
it wants to own her breasts,
dream about spreading
its wings.

She's angry at the malice
of bruises that crowd
her arms like flower buds,
gaudy shades of purple,
green, yellow.

And she's growing tired
of the middle and wonders
how it will end, weary of that face
with dark socketed eyes
straining to see the impossible.

But the sky turns cerulean blue,
heaven blue, and hope
puts down a tiny root
even as a poppy bruise
flowers around the I.V.

Cancer School

enrollment
is involuntary
with few rules
teacher says
light up with rays
and get a X for
the course
you can shoot-up
with an approved
substance and eat
in class any time
as long as it's pills
that infiltrate ears
nose toes and nerves
pain and numbness
fight to be
your best friend
and if you
can't eat
your nickname
will be Skinny
if you throw up
or soil panties
no one will call
your parents
HOPE is the
bulletin board buzz word
REMISSION
lets you graduate
smile for the camera

After He Left

If her heart were the sun, it would wrap the stars around it like a shawl
    to stay warm.

If her heart were the moon, it would pull the shade and turn out the light.

If her heart had a mouth, it would be tempted to feed its starved self on
    the pretty golden mushrooms growing in the woods, taking a
    chance like Tsar Alexis.

If her heart were a flower, it would bloom too late and wander lost in deep
    snow.

If her heart were a landscape, drought would steal the creek's heartbeat
    and lick the ground's lips until they cracked.

If her heart had eyes, it would look out the window to watch for
    thunderheads and when the rains came, it could fall in love again.

Young Boys Watch Helentroy Diamond Jones

It's the perfect cupid's bow of her upper lip
when she smiles, the way her breasts
mock modesty, how honey suckle fragrance
seduces the breeze as she passes. And those
hips riding high, swaying in a pretty rhythm.

In daydreams, they stop her,
slide the straps of the white eyelet dress
off those slender shoulders, whiteness
wound around each finger, they touch
the dangerous white skin under the soft cloth.

Her white legs flare against the night sky
and stir up a whiteness that lights the boys'
eyes and tongues, filling their loins,
they hold the whiteness in their hands
as it rises into the black air.

Francisco Goya, Don Manuel Osorio de Zuniga

Viewed at night, the cats disappear
into the canvas. The three of them stalk
in the shadows, deadly intent reflected
in their eyes. I see just an unsmiling boy
dressed in scarlet and lace, who poses
with his pet magpie, out of its cage
and near his feet.

Something is amiss.
Has he angered his mother?
Perhaps she will call him into the garden
where yesterday he cut all the scarlet tulips
that had ignited the hill. She will hold
his hand and raise the scarlet sleeve, kiss
a crimson bruise on his arm with her red pomade,
leaving a flower, the red thrum pressed against
his lips, such an indelible red, as though it were
painted on with a brush.

Weather Alert

The all-nighter ends
and a red sky urges
Daddy to kick open
the front door.

He's all cranked up on
too much whiskey-rage,
his fists hell-bent,
Ma falls to the floor,
her ribs aching,
a ritual she can't stop.

We kids hide
In the bedroom back
by the window box,
our teary-eyed talk
lacks sound, words
brood in a crowd
of rag dolls, books and trucks.

Later a red sky night
will sprinkle sweet
quiet delight like a row
of red-cheeked apricots
ripening on the window sill.

It's always the same
the same the same
token of "sorry"
that can't tell itself
from not enough shame.

The Binge Drinker's Daughter

Once again his voice punches and slaps
the night awake. Sleep struggles
to keep the anger and whiskey breath
from stealing the air when suddenly
the loudness cuffs her into the corner.
Fear races up her spine. Thoughts,
cold and black as the fireplace poker
with its curved, deadly point she wants
to stab into his chest, flow into the rooms
of her heart.

She waits, shivering on the floor.
Something about dawn, how it will fling
its arms around night's chill and pick
the lock of the nightmare to let the shadows out.

The Large Baby Doll: 1956

When I die, Hallelujah, by and by, I'll fly away.
When the shadows of this life have gone, I'll fly away
Like a bird from prison bars has flown, I'll fly away
Hymn by Alfred E. Bromley

Sue is the nuns' baby,
a three-year-old foundling
with a perfect doll's face,
gold hair and blue eyes
but she has a genetic defect—
she has no muscle tone,
was born a "floppy baby."

Beautiful Sue who has
an underdeveloped brain,
webbed fingers and toes,
lives in a small room off
the pediatric ward, one of
the Sisters' charity cases.

At St. Luke's every day
one of us nurses brush
Sue's hair into Shirley Temple
curls and carefully feed her,
and if she should choke,
we flip her over and give
back slaps until she breathes.

It's sad Sue will never play
hopscotch, fall in love or
sew on a button.
How it will end, no one knows,
But I wish she could escape
that dull space before a choking
spell terrifies lungs into a hopeless
struggle for air.

I imagine her flying up
into the sky on her webbed
fingers and toes, her milky skin
covered with the moon's
silvery silk threads and laughing
out loud for the first time.

2 West

On 2 West, the pediatric
leukemia ward where
Remission and Relapse
fight a lethal duel, my nurse's
plan of care is full of nursery
rhymes and lullabies.

On 2 West in a room
where everyone is gowned,
gloved and masked,
I rock a baby, the parents
are standing behind me,
crying. I rock and rock,
grief gathering around
my chair which I can't escape
so I keep on rocking, my mask
getting wetter and wetter.

Ypsilanti State Mental Hospital, 1951

> *Ypsilanti State Hospital was closed in 1991. At its peak in the 1950s it housed 4000 patients.*

1. Vamping

The student nurses were not allowed
on Ward 7, but we were curious,
so we squirted ample Evening in Paris,
on wrists, backs of ears, some between
our breasts, then flattered the male
attendants, who grinned and unlocked the doors.

Once inside the smell of piss and shit
and disinfectant smacked our noses
rushing us to the day room where yelling
from schizophrenics created a din,
but the loudest sound was the attendants'
guffaws as we dodged the lobotomy patients,

young men who were trying to touch
our arms, hair, faces. *I want to leave with
you,* one said, *I used to be bad, but the doc
fixed my brain. Look. See the scar?
I want the hell out and I want to feel
some girls where they smell pretty like you.*

2. Hydrotherapy

The patient paces chatters
nonstop hasn't slept in three nights
declares herself a queen
smears lipstick on cheeks and lips
some on a sanitary napkin
she knows what's coming
> *see I'm on my period*
> *can't get in the tub*
> *I want my red skirt*
> *where are my boulevard shoes*

three attendants all female muscle
through double-locked doors
their strength overpowers
arms and legs fighting back
into the tub room into the tub
> *where are my boulevard shoes*

a canvas restraint holds her down like nails
the cold water pries between thighs
held tight then forces itself up to her neck
the queen's skin shivering white
so cold she's sobbing
> *my boulevard shoes*
> *my boulevard shoes*

3. Treatment Plan
> *The use of lobotomies, a form of psychosurgery, increased from the early 1940s to the mid- 1950s when antipsychotic medications were introduced. Its use has been abandoned.*

Take a young man,
include his behavior.
Measure the homework
he refuses to do, the classes
he skips and the words *fuck*
and *bitch* he utters daily. Next,
add two cups of his parents' rage,
though I recommend you cover
your ears while they beat him
with a leather belt. Combine
ingredients in a pot and simmer
while folding in the comic books
he steals from the newsstand.

When the mixture begins to boil,
quickly thicken with juvenile court
and commitment papers,
being careful to skim off pleas
of *Wait, no, I can change.*
Now hold down the young man
on the table and truss his arms
and legs. Lift the upper eyelids
and insert long metal skewers
and scramble the frontal lobe
into a savory dish of obedience.

4. Jesus Catches the Light in His Hands

Ralph, a slight man,
believes he becomes
Jesus himself
when he cups his hands
and catches a beam of sunlight
darting across the wall
refracted by someone's ring.

In the instant he is born again,
benches and chairs fly around
the day room as if on wings
then spit thunder
when they splinter on the floor.
Afterwards, he crawls into a corner
and sleeps.

He does this because years ago
syphilis bacteria from an infected whore
chewed holes his brain
and left behind the grandiose delusion
with nothing to do except try
to slip out of those holes at every chance
and mate with the rays of light.

The Open Window

The memory is powered by the scent
of incense in church—
I'm sixteen again in my hour
of Adoration at St. Ann's.
The wooden kneeler is exacting
penance from my skinny knees,
the stained glass window is open
and a startling, sapphire blue sky
rushes in stealing my attention.

Someone's glass rosary beads
chinkle, reminding me to pray,
but it's 6 a.m. and my mind wanders.
I notice lilies on the altar, love
how their breath surrounds me,
then think of the boy who stuck
his tongue in my mouth when
we kissed on the front porch.
I worry it was a sin. I didn't like
his warm spit, though I liked kissing,
the way he pulled me close
and hugged so tight I could feel
his hardness.

One lit votive candle on the table
in front of my pew flickers,
resurrecting its red glow. Contrite,
I light another, hope I'll be forgiven
before the breeze from the window
can put out the flame.

Riding a Red Bicycle

A woman of uncertain age lies in her bedroom
in perfect darkness where not even the porch light
can press hard enough against the window to enter.

She begins to dream—she is riding a red bicycle
through town wearing nothing but bright color-
changing bra and panties—tangerine to cobalt blue

to sherbet green. She feels as real as the incandescent horse
that lives in Oz. In the morning she records the dream
determined not to lose it like the dream the night before.

That one was as fragile as a violet. One petal dried up
as she made the coffee, another as she watched a ruby-
throated humming bird outside the kitchen window.

The rest wilted when she fell in love with the dip
and loop of a black butterfly showing off in the back yard.
Does it matter what dreams mean? What they tell her

is all she can know, that she can dress up in perfect
darkness and hold night in the cup of her hand.

No Exit

I never want to die
but if I do
I'll come back as a cloud
If it loses steam
or stages a storm
I'll pack up and go on vacation
as a raindrop and visit the ocean
I won't need a ticket
to ride the waves and when
I get bored I'll lie on the sand
Feet will kick me free
and I'll fly up on a sun ray
to live as a bright new cloud
When it rains I'll piggy-back down
land on your nose
look you in the eye and you'll say
oh—I remember you

Carbon
      after Michelle Boisseau

I am carbon. I am everywhere.
I am in the air you breathe, the gas in your car,
in the muck, in fizzy cocktails, on your mother's grave,
the stub of your cigarette, spine of the Bible.
I have been buried deep, deformed, tightly folded,
eroded, uplifted, weathered and sheared.
I am the dream of gemologists: blood diamond,
 black diamond, coral and pearl.
I make girls happy with my dazzle when they raise
their finger showing off a ring.
I hear laughter when children hold their sticks
tipped with marshmallows over my fire. I am the disaster
in coal miners' lungs, the joke of climate-change doubters,
the poisonous partner with oxygen, the dirty face
of the moon.
We take each other for granted, the two of us,
now and forever, but we are as close as the speck
in your left eye. I am the grit on your shoes,
the smudge on the tasseled lamp, the soot
on the sill where I lurk, waiting to fly.

Persistence, 1956

My euonymus bush
ran out of beauty
so each morning for a week
I straddled it, drove my shovel
in circles to loosen the roots,
cursing and sweating,
yanking and pulling,
but it hung on for dear life.

Once a woman miscarried
on my shift. Suddenly,
it lay between her legs,
smaller than imaginable,
red, raw. Faint cheeps
echoed from under the tent
of sheets. The doctor's
agitated finger couldn't hush up
the miniature mouth.
Get it out of here, he hissed.

I wrapped baby and placenta
in a towel and ran to the utility room
where time hunkered around
the tiny life as it tried to lay down roots.

The sun shines on a bruised
yard now that the bush
is gone. It's left with a hole,
deep but not too wide, useful
for burying something small.
I'm telling you this to say
I know about hanging on.

Broken, 1970

The Body Is The Temple Of The Soul
(Sign above the Autopsy Room door)

On the cancer ward where
after surgery body parts disappear
leaving stick heads without
jawbones, throat parts,
where a goose neck lamp
sets aglow their emptiness
when the dressing comes off,

where the nurse's knees
turn weak the first time
she sees just half a face,
where desperate eyes
are dulled by a deserting sun,
where life slides down
to the quiet stage,

where a pathologist
sits on a patient's bed,
probing, *where does it hurt,*
but never telling her by week's
end in the autopsy room
it will be *his* hands cutting up
her body, coaxing out its secrets,

on the cancer ward
where Death, like a con man
takes a little, a little more,
sneaking away a person piece
by piece.

Sailor
for Lee

He sleeps fitfully in the easy chair, his bronze skin
radiant in the early morning light.

His life now a tiresome thing, so he busies himself
untying the strings that hold him to it. His fingers fumble

and cannot undo the last knot. There's no time left
for talk. Yesterday all his words departed like a flock

of startled gulls. Today he concentrates
on each breath, its depth and volume,

as if tuning a motor, precisely gauging
the richness of oxygen, just how much

is needed to fend off drowning in the waters
that balloon legs and belly.

Each spring he'd leave the cherry farm to ship out
on the Great Lakes freighters until hell froze over—

twenty-one days on, ten days off and back to the farm.
For too long he lived this double life without a vacation

and never complained, even when a late frost wrecked
the entire crop. No running away then or now.

Knives, chemicals, radiation have taken aim, but none
hit deep enough. He calms himself by puckering

his lips for a kiss from his elder daughter. Tonight
we will stand watch with him, hold hands and ask

ourselves what choice do any of us have—who can refuse
one last kiss, the one that makes us hold our breath and wait.

Mad Red Sunset

Carrie's father is dying
so she wants to sell the cabin
and fly to some new place
where he could bird-watch.
He says, *No, no, I've said goodbye
to that life.*

Then he tells her what bird
he'd like to see one more time—
the elusive scarlet tanager,
describing it as a flash
of madder red tricked out in feathers
and black wings.
Suddenly he grimaces,
as though angry with himself.
It's as if he had just confessed
to wanting a million dollars.
He agrees to a poster print
of a tanager and wants it tacked
over his bed to take care of him
while he sleeps—he laughs—
as if it were a guardian angel.

Will Carrie's father soon sleep,
see black wing-beats and an upward
curve of red stunning the air?

The Heart Rate You See on the Monitor May Not Be Accurate

If only a heart could curl, press,
extend and crunch, then wipe away
the sweat after working its way
back to hammer strength.

My mother died of heart failure.
Death shadowed her so slowly
that my grief knotted up like sore
muscles.

I married the peacock of men.
Before his heart ran away
he wore out *my* heart using it
as a mirror and fell in love with himself.

My heart has cooled down. It has earned
countless calluses and when one of them
ruptures sleep, I'm happy just to lie
with the moon and keep her company.

In a Perfect World

I would love you in summer when a parade
of Queen Ann's Lace stands at attention
along the path where we walk and you wouldn't
look skyward and let dreams eat your words.

And I would love you in autumn when leaves
take off their green and the air is almost palpable
with red- gold- plum and you wouldn't stare
at the creek, waiting to watch your image

smile back. What's the use of wanting anything
if I can't love you in winter when snow steals
the show, muffling sound so not even a handclap
can be heard. You would never clap your hands

over your ears while I sing to you in spring,
softly repeating my song like the bluebird
busy flying back and forth from the pine tree
collecting needles, the song walking with you

and ribbons of moonlight touching your shoulders.
You certainly wouldn't brush aside the light,
say it's too heavy and isn't it time to let spring fall
behind our eyes. Would you?

Sometimes a Body Is Just a Body

Breasts don't write to cancer and say I wish you were here, but if bone marrow grows bored, don't think it won't pump itself up and dance, attracting curious cancer cells that will stop by uninvited.

Feeling melancholy is not a sin as long as you do penance by rescuing moonbeams dead-ended on your pillow.

Heap imagination around you, sit in its lap and don't let age wear it out.

Hypochondriacs wrap their arm around their complaints. The complaints put on mascara and rhinestone earrings and dream they're the life of the party.

Capture the images playing tag with your sleep and then let them stretch and run in every direction.

I want to teach my body patience when my muscles get mad at me for not moving but all I want to do is sit all day inhabiting a poem.

Bodies are not created equal. Some break out in a sweat looking at an unfinished poem.
Some break out in a sweat when a blank piece of paper pulls their eyes into a garden where there is no rain.

Sometimes a body is just a place to live.

The Drums Argue

Once again sleep
is too small a space
to fall into.
Her eyes pay attention
to the dark as she wonders
why black is so black
and what has she done
to deserve so much of it.

Sometimes she listens
to all-night jazz
but often the tenor sax
craves dissonance
and the drums argue.

She envies the trees.
Their branches understand
the thickness of wind,
still themselves and fall asleep.

She longs for a column
of moonlight shimmering
in the underbelly of night
where she crawls into sleep,
gently, like a leaf falling,
a soft drum-roll fading out.

Saying I'm Sorry after the Quarrel

If I could fall out of this life,
I would live as a chicory flower
on the sidewalk in a crack.
I would raise my head
as you passed by,
hoping you'd listen to the music
of my dark blue loveliness,
notes floating up around you
like bold perfume.

I have just one day to live.
Each minute wants to stretch
like a rainbow, resisting the clock
to cling like a vine, its blossoms
leaning on your shoulder
whispering about my sweetness.
If I'm lucky, desire will follow you,
and as you sleep, lift your lids
and kiss your dream on the mouth.

Migraine

The pain in my left temple
has unpacked and settled in,
quickly becoming jealous
of friends, books, the garden,
wants me to hold it
in my arms while giving me
a barbed kiss,
wants to sleep on my pillow,
squalling like a baby until
I sing it to sleep,
wants to sit at the table to steal
my broth, help itself to a glass
of my Chardonnay and thief that it is,
wants to look through my eyes
so it can steal the pain pill
before I even unscrew the cap.

Hand-Speaking
> *for my daughter Peggy*

Peggy teaches little ones
whose only words are those
their fingers know—
like gathering the fingers
of one hand to make an "O"
then touching the left side
of the nose, then the right
signs *flower*,
a finger running down
the cheek signs *tears*,
or a finger rotating on the cheek,
apple. Her hands curving
through the air tell words
the way ballet dancers tell stories.

But hand-speaking a poem
is done with her whole body—
shoulders sway, the waist stretches
and flows into an arabesque,
upper limbs perform a *pas de deux,*
and for those few moments,
her space is a dancery.

I Was Going to Write

About a coral scarf caught in barbed wire
waving to us as we passed, then the farmer
in a pig truck who shook his fist at the woman
tending the vegetable stand. I thought I'd mention
that the scream of a frightened pig can measure
115 decibels, more powerful than that of a jet
taking off at 113 decibels.

Other things came to mind to tell you,
such as the woman who suffers rheumatoid
arthritis saying, *Sometimes my hands and feet
shout with pain.* I heard of a large pterosaur
that walked on all fours, the wings folded down
to become legs and feet. Then there was a dream
I had about flowers that could talk.

The poppies trying to shoot the moon
in their little red voices, the daffodils content
to hum and sun themselves, the pinks whispering
to each other and the petunias merely sighing .
I wanted to tell you the last time you said my name
a grave blanket of wildflowers drowned out the sound.

And after that I couldn't think of anything else to say.

Mary Sesso was born Mary Carolyn Muehlmann and grew up in Michigan. She attended the Mercy School of Nursing, worked as a registered nurse until retirement and now sits on the Human Rights Committee at the National Children's Center. She holds a BA from the University of Maryland and an MFA from Vermont College. She is a member of the Writer's Center in Bethesda, Maryland, and is active in three poetry workshops. Her most recent work appeared in the *Coal Hill Review, Chest, Comstock Review, Helen Literary Magazine, Passager, The Medical Literary Messenger* and the *Gyroscope Review*.

www.ingramcontent.com/pod-product-compliance
Lightning Source LLC
LaVergne TN
LVHW041604070426
835507LV00011B/1306